FOR MY DAUGHTER VITTORIA

COPYRIGHT © 2016, ELENA BIASIN

ALL RIGHTS RESERVED

MAYA & GAIA

A SPECIAL BIRTHDAY

ELENA BIASIN

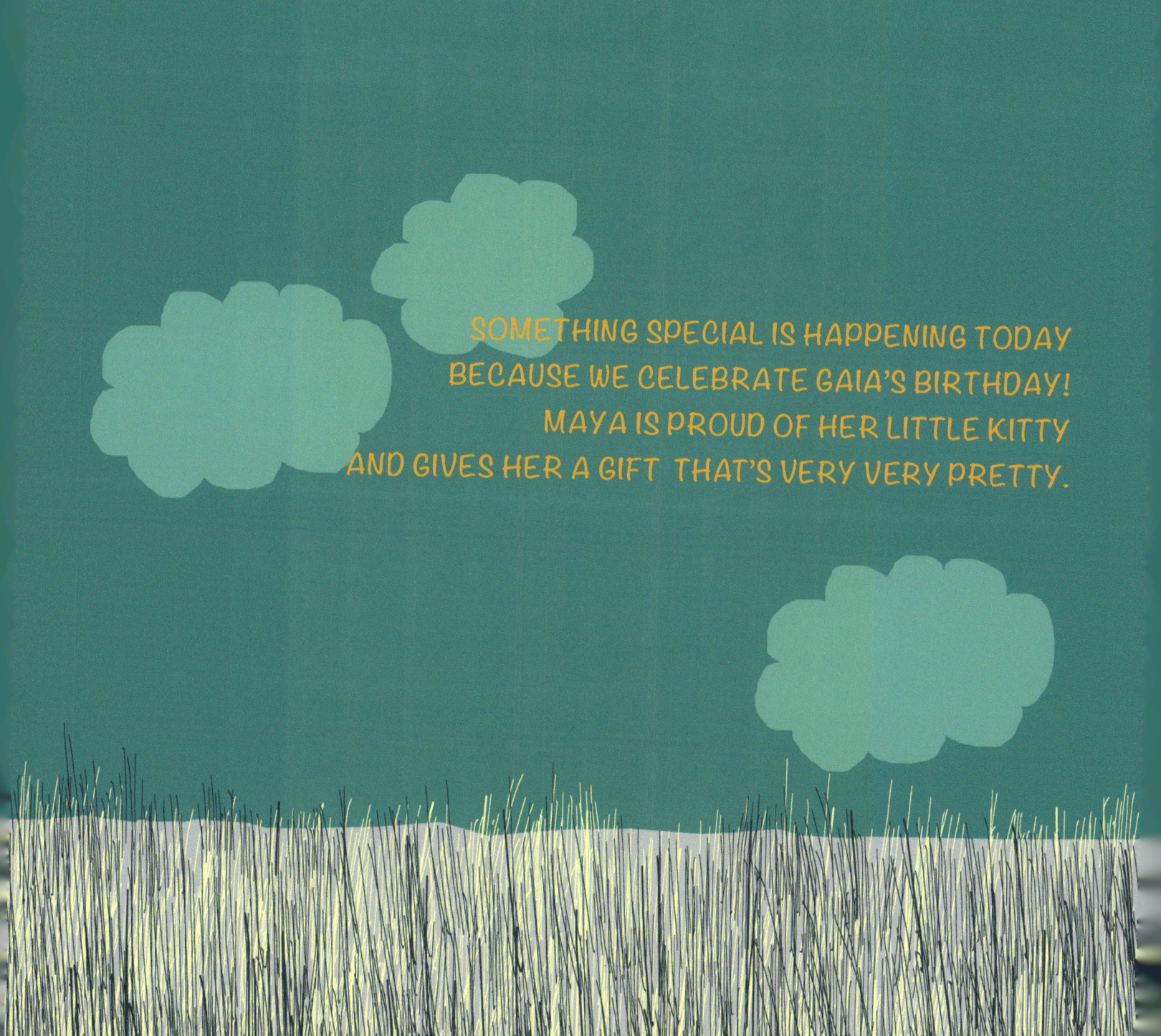

A HUGE BOX! AND WHAT DOES IT LOOK LIKE?
GAIA PEEKS INSIDE TO FIND A YELLOW BIKE!

THEY JUMP ON THE BIKE AND COAST THE HILL DOWN
THEY RIDE AND EXPLORE THEIR QUAINT LITTLE TOWN.
LEFT AND RIGHT THEY PEDAL SO FAST;
HOUSES, GARDENS AND TREES FLY PAST!

FINALLY THEY REACH THE TOWN'S GREEN WOODS;
UNDER THE TREES LIE SUCCULENT GOODS.

STRAWBERRIES, BLUEBERRIES, MUSHROOMS AND MINT;
OF VIOLETS AND MOSS, THEY SMELL A HINT!

RIGHT THROUGH THE TREES A BRIGHT, SHINY LAKE
A HOME TO SWANS AND GEESE IT MAKES.

RIDING THE BIKE THEY MEET THE SHORE;
TIME FOR THEIR PICNIC WITH BREAD, FRUIT AND MORE!

IN THE BLINK OF AN EYE FROM THE WATER APPEARS
THE DRAGON OF THE LAKE WHICH EVERYBODY FEARS.

HIS TEETH ARE SO LONG, AND SO SHARP AND SO WHITE, HIS MOUTH IS SO LARGE, A WHOLE PIE HE CAN BITE!

MAYA AND GAIA RUN SWIFTLY AWAY;
FRIGHTENED AND TREMBLING ...THEY CANNOT STAY.

THE DRAGON CRIES OUT, "IS ANYONE THERE?"
FROM HIS WIDE MOUTH, FIRE DOES FLARE.

THE PORCUPINE SQUEEZES UNDER A BUSH,
THE MOLE SCRAMBLES INTO HIS HOLE WITH A PUSH.
BEHIND THE TREE BRANCHES HIDES A BROWN OWL;
NO ANIMAL HAZARDS A SOUND OR A GROWL.

MAYA AND GAIA HOLD THEMSELVES TIGHT;
IF THEY DON'T MOVE THEY WILL BE ALL RIGHT.
THE DRAGON FEELS LONELY, SAD AND DESPISED;
TWO LARGE TEAR DROPS FALL FROM HIS EYES.

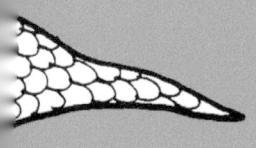

MAYA AND GAIA CREEPING CLOSE BY
QUIETLY ASK HIM, "WHY DO YOU CRY?".
SOBBING AND SIGHING THE DRAGON REPLIES,
"I HAVE NO FRIENDS, IS THAT A SURPRISE?
EVERYONE FEARS MY LOOKS AND MY FIRE
BUT I CAN DO MANY DEEDS YOU'D ADMIRE."

"YOU MAY LOOK DIFFERENT, BUT THAT'S UNDERSTOOD;
WE NOW KNOW THAT YOU WANT TO BE GOOD.
WE ARE YOUR FRIENDS, LET'S HAVE A BALL;
ALL FOR ONE AND ONE FOR ALL!"

THE WOOD IS THEIR PLAYGROUND THIS BRIGHT, SUNNY DAY;
THEY SING, THEY DANCE, THEY TALK AND THEY PLAY.

ARRIVING BACK HOME, TOGETHER THEY BAKE
GAIA'S OWN FAVOURITE BIRTHDAY CAKE.
THE DRAGON THEN ADDS HIS OWN LITTLE TOUCH
WITH HIS FIERY FIRE HE CAN DO SO MUCH.
HE LIGHTS THE CANDLES ONE BY ONE;
HAPPY BIRTHDAY, HAVE LOTS OF FUN!

www.ingramcontent.com/pod-product-compliance
Lightning Source LLC
Chambersburg PA
CBHW041406010526
44107CB00015B/1091